Maurice Pledger's

Dinosaur World

sticker book

With over 150 reusable stickers!

A sticker adventure back in time...

templar publishing

What are dinosaurs?

Have you ever seen a real, live dinosaur? Actually, no one has, because dinosaurs became extinct (they died out) around 65 million years ago! Scientists can still tell a lot about them though, from ancient remains called fossils…

The first dinosaurs began to appear about 230 million years ago… They survived on earth for over 160 million years!

The time in which dinosaurs lived is divided into three different stages: the Triassic, Jurassic, and Cretaceous.
Look at the timeline opposite to see what came 'before' and 'after' the dinosaurs…

mya = million years ago

Before dinosaurs… 540 to 248 mya
540 – 500 mya: The Age of Trilobites
505 – 438 mya: First corals, seaweed & land plants
438 – 408 mya: First insects
408 – 360 mya: The Age of Fishes
360 – 325 mya: First winged insects
325 – 280 mya: First reptiles, mayflies & cockroaches
280 – 248 mya: The Age of Amphibians

'Dinosaur' means 'terrible lizard'! Be prepared, you will meet lots of them in this book, along with flying reptiles called pterosaurs, and giant marine creatures. Can you bring them back to life? Turn to the back of the book where you'll find lots of stickers, which you can use to complete the activities throughout!

TIMELINE

**Triassic period
248 to 208 mya**
First dinosaurs, mammals & prehistoric crocodiles

**Jurassic period
208 to 146 mya**
Sauropods, first birds, pterosaurs & ammonites

**Cretaceous period
146 to 65 mya**
146 – 98 mya: Dinosaurs in Full Swing!
98 – 65 mya: 'Tale-end' of the Dinosaurs…

**After dinosaurs…
65 mya to present day**
The Age of Mammals

Dinosaur types

Dinosaurs came in all shapes and sizes. But they were not the only reptiles on the planet all those years ago… Two of the reptiles opposite are not dinosaurs – can you tell who? Fill in the shapes with the colourful stickers from the back of your book.

Apatosaurus

This was a plant-eating dinosaur that walked on all four legs. An adult *Apatosaurus* could be up to 27 metres long. Like other dinosaurs, it laid eggs and the baby hatched from one that was around 30 centimetres wide.

Ceratosaurus

Ceratosaurus was a meat-eating dinosaur that walked upright on its back legs and attacked other dinosaurs. It had three small horns on its head but its real weapons were its fearsome claws and its 70 giant, razor-sharp teeth!

Apatosaurus

Ceratosaurus

4

Tyrannosaurus (dinosaur)

Compsognathus (dinosaur)

Stegosaurus (dinosaur)

Diplodocus (dinosaur)

Ceratosaurus (dinosaur)

Pteradactylus (pterosaur)

Liopleurodon (marine reptile)

Triceratops (dinosaur)

Turn over to find a scene to use your stickers on

Release your new dinosaur friends (big and small) into the desert below and see how they get along!

Turn to the STICKER FUN section at the back of this book
to find even more dinosaurs you can add to this picture.

7

Terrible theropods

Theropods were meat-eating dinosaurs that stood on their back legs. They had long tails, which they used for balance when running. Some were small and very quick, while others made the earth tremble when they moved!

Velociraptor

A ferocious fighter, this quick-mover would jump towards its victim, attacking with dagger-like claws on its back legs.

Troodon

This highly intelligent hunter was larger than *Velociraptor*. It had an unusually large brain for its size, making it the smartest theropod.

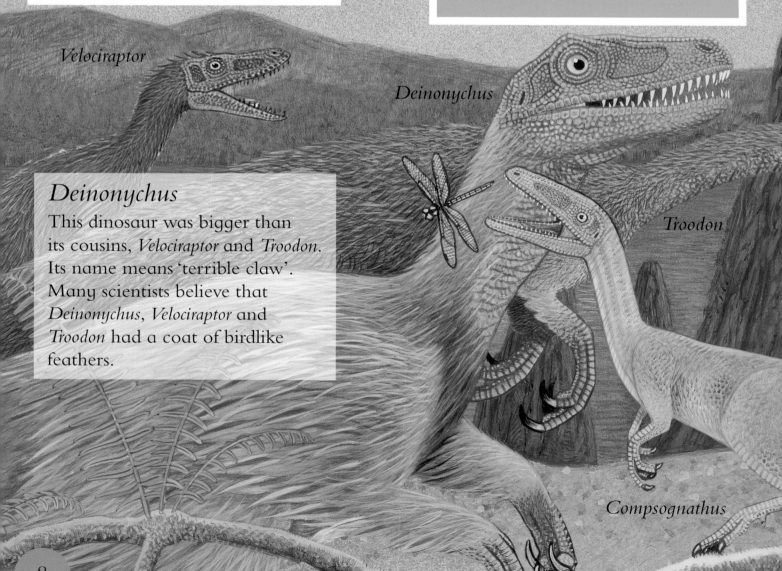

Deinonychus

This dinosaur was bigger than its cousins, *Velociraptor* and *Troodon*. Its name means 'terrible claw'. Many scientists believe that *Deinonychus*, *Velociraptor* and *Troodon* had a coat of birdlike feathers.

Velociraptor

Deinonychus

Troodon

Compsognathus

Tyrannosaurus

One of the largest theropods, *Tyrannosaurus* had a head over a metre long with a large brain – making it not only an extremely big and terrifying hunter, but also a very clever one!

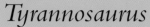

Dilophosaurus

This strong dinosaur would hunt in a pack with other members of its family. It had two bony crowns on its head, which were probably used to attract a mate.

Tyrannosaurus

Compsognathus

As small as a cat, *Compsognathus* hunted like one too, using its sharp eyesight and speed to catch large insects or lizards.

Dilophosaurus

Mighty meat-eaters

The meat-eaters were the most frightening of all the dinosaurs. The smallest ones preyed on creatures, such as insects, but the bigger, stronger meat-eaters would attack animals much larger than themselves, including other dinosaurs!

Coelophysis

These dinosaurs lived in the desert and were up to 3 metres long. They hunted as a pack, which helped them to kill bigger creatures. They were also quick enough to gobble up small lizards.

Eoraptor

Coelophysis

Herrerasaurus

Allosaurus

Albertosaurus

Velociraptor

Giganotosaurus

Sinosauropteryx

Compsognathus

What the meat-eaters ate

How do we know what meat-eating dinosaurs ate? Scientists are able to tell what a dinosaur had for dinner by examining the fossilised remains in its stomach.

Diplodocus

Apatosaurus

Vegetarian monsters

There were many different types of plant-eating dinosaur, including armoured ones like *Stegosaurus* and *Styracosaurus*. The largest dinosaurs that ever lived were known as sauropods – they walked on all four legs, and had very long necks and tails. Can you spot the sauropods on this page?

Parasaurolophus

Allosaurus

Sauropods were always on the alert for prowling predators, such as vicious *Allosaurus*. This meat-eater used its claws to cling onto its victims and its jaws could open extra wide to take massive bites!

Apatosaurus

Although not the largest of the sauropods, *Apatosaurus* weighed as much as four elephants, and never stopped eating!

Diplodocus

Measuring up to 27 metres long, this sauropod could rear up on its back legs, using its long neck to reach the highest leaves. It could also reach down to eat underwater plants on river beds, using its tail for balance.

What the plant-eaters ate

As well as looking at the fossilised contents of dinosaurs' stomachs, scientists study fossilised dinosaur droppings, called coprolites, to find out what these reptiles ate. A plant-eater's poo contains traces of seeds or leaves, while a meat-eater's has bits of bone.

Stegosaurus

Styracosaurus

Thecodontosaurus

This was one of the first plant-eating dinosaurs to walk the earth. It was only 2 metres long and walked mainly on its back legs.

Peaceful plant-eaters

What do you think of when someone mentions the word 'dinosaur'? Gnashing jaws full of ferocious, dagger-like teeth? That's certainly what some of the big meat-eaters looked like, but the peaceful plant-eaters needed jaws and teeth that could munch through plants instead of tearing meat apart.

Saurolophus

Saurolophus was another duck-billed dinosaur, with jaws perfectly designed for ripping and chewing plants. It also had a bony crest at the back of its skull, which scientists believe it may have used to make a noise and attract others in its herd.

Maiasaura

Maiasaura had a flat beak – ideal for nibbling tough plants. It is known as a hadrosaur, or duck-billed dinosaur.

Brachiosaurus

Sauroposeidon

Supersaurus

Mamenchisaurus

Edmontosaurus

Diplodocus

Iguanodon

Iguanodon could stand on two legs or four and had large spikes on its front feet, which it used to gather food and to defend itself. Scientists studying *Iguanodon* fossils first thought that the spikes were horns that grew out of its head.

Prehistoric plants

The first plants began to appear on land about 430 million years ago – 200 million years before the first dinosaurs. These plants were very small and grew only near the coast, but by the time the dinosaurs ruled the earth there were forests of trees, shrubs and ferns where they could feed and hunt.

Ferns

Ferns first appeared around 360 million years ago and are among the world's oldest plants. During the dinosaur age there were different types of fern, some only knee-high and some up to 20 metres tall!

Trees

Fir trees, willow trees and ginkgo trees that we would recognise today all existed during the time of the dinosaurs. Trees even grew near the South Pole, although it was far warmer there than it is today.

Flowers

Flowering plants have existed for up to 130 million years. If you could transport yourself back to the end of the dinosaur age you would see flowers like wild roses and magnolias.

Turn over to find a scene to use your stickers on

Turn to the STICKER FUN ___ ion to find your favourite dinosaurs ___ forest.

Ready for battle

The theropod hunters were well-equipped warriors with teeth and claws, but the dinosaurs they attacked knew how to protect themselves. Can you find the stickers for each of the brave dinosaurs shown opposite? Check out their body armour, spikes and clubs!

Nodosaurus

Nodosaurus had no weapons to defend itself. Instead, just like a hedgehog curls up to show its spines, it would hug the ground so that only the bony plates on its back and sides would show.

Euoplocephalus

This large dinosaur had tough spikes on its head and body to ward off attackers. It also had a heavy bone club in its tail for whacking enemies.

Kentrosaurus

Saichania

Ankylosaurus

Scelidosaurus

Edmontonia

Leptoceratops

Horns, spikes and spines

The largest sauropods could stomp on a smaller predator and the heavy, swishing tail of *Diplodocus* could easily kill an attacker, but the smaller plant-eaters had to use armour including horns, spikes and spines to protect themselves. Can you think of any animals today that use horns to scare away enemies?

Stegosaurus

With two rows of armour plates running down its back, *Stegosaurus* was a very awkward creature to attack. It also had some nasty spikes in its tail to use as weapons.

Stegosaurus

Styracosaurus

Stegosaurus

Styracosaurus

A spiky shield protected the skull and neck of this dinosaur, while it used its long nose-horn to fight off attackers.

Boneheads

Without proper horns to defend themselves, some dinosaurs, like *Pachycephalosaurus* (shown here) had to use their heads — as battering rams! Their skulls were nearly 25 centimetres thick!

Protoceratops

Protoceratops

The powerful beak and jaws of *Protoceratops* could give any attacker a painful bite, while an armoured frill protected its neck. *Protoceratops* was only the size of a big dog, but it lived in large herds for extra safety.

Leptoceratops

Leptoceratops

Similar in size to *Protoceratops*, these dinosaurs also had sharp, parrot-like beaks and armoured frills. If these failed to scare enemies, they could run away quickly.

Triceratops

Triceratops

About the size of an elephant, *Triceratops* had a spiked frill for protection and three large horns on its head to fight with. Some scientists also believe that it may have had sharp spines like a porcupine.

Record breakers

Dinosaurs were the tallest, longest, heaviest animals ever to walk the earth. Some were as big as a house and three times longer than a bus! Yet dinosaurs are not the largest creatures ever to have lived. The largest creatures on the planet are still alive today. Do you know what they are? Read on to find out…

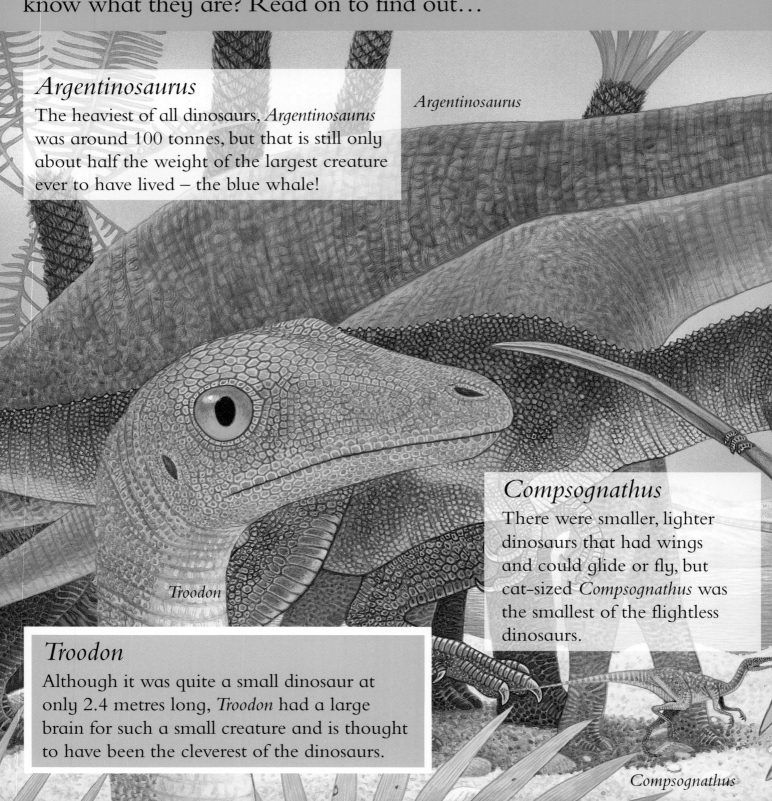

Argentinosaurus

The heaviest of all dinosaurs, *Argentinosaurus* was around 100 tonnes, but that is still only about half the weight of the largest creature ever to have lived – the blue whale!

Argentinosaurus

Compsognathus

There were smaller, lighter dinosaurs that had wings and could glide or fly, but cat-sized *Compsognathus* was the smallest of the flightless dinosaurs.

Troodon

Troodon

Although it was quite a small dinosaur at only 2.4 metres long, *Troodon* had a large brain for such a small creature and is thought to have been the cleverest of the dinosaurs.

Compsognathus

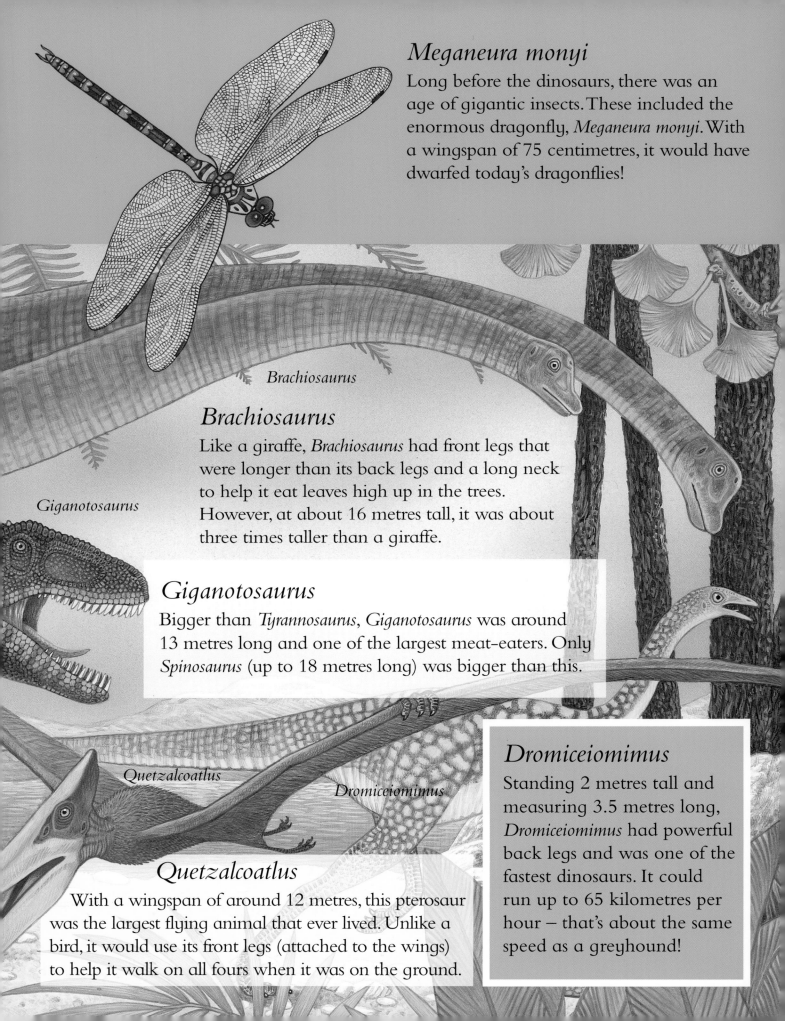

Meganeura monyi

Long before the dinosaurs, there was an age of gigantic insects. These included the enormous dragonfly, *Meganeura monyi*. With a wingspan of 75 centimetres, it would have dwarfed today's dragonflies!

Brachiosaurus

Brachiosaurus

Like a giraffe, *Brachiosaurus* had front legs that were longer than its back legs and a long neck to help it eat leaves high up in the trees. However, at about 16 metres tall, it was about three times taller than a giraffe.

Giganotosaurus

Giganotosaurus

Bigger than *Tyrannosaurus*, *Giganotosaurus* was around 13 metres long and one of the largest meat-eaters. Only *Spinosaurus* (up to 18 metres long) was bigger than this.

Quetzalcoatlus

Dromiceiomimus

Dromiceiomimus

Standing 2 metres tall and measuring 3.5 metres long, *Dromiceiomimus* had powerful back legs and was one of the fastest dinosaurs. It could run up to 65 kilometres per hour – that's about the same speed as a greyhound!

Quetzalcoatlus

With a wingspan of around 12 metres, this pterosaur was the largest flying animal that ever lived. Unlike a bird, it would use its front legs (attached to the wings) to help it walk on all fours when it was on the ground.

Noisy noisy dinosaurs

You might think that all dinosaurs roared or growled, but some could make all sorts of strange calls. The hadrosaurs – also known as duckbills – had a range of crests, horns and tubes on their heads. Just as an elephant can trumpet using its trunk, these plant-eating dinosaurs could use their musical instruments to hoot, honk or bellow, and communicate with their herd!

Lambeosaurus

Lambeosaurus

One of the biggest duckbills, *Lambeosaurus* blew air from its nose and into its hollow axe-shaped crest to make a honk or toot sound.

Parasaurolophus

Parasaurolophus

These dinosaurs could make a whistling or trumpeting noise through the hollow crest on their heads.

Anatotitan

Anatotitan would blow up the loose skin around its nostrils to make a loud croaking or belching noise.

Anatotitan

Corythosaurus

The plate-shaped crest of *Corythosaurus* contained a complicated pattern of hollow passages that it could use to make a deep, booming bellow.

Corythosaurus

Oviraptor

It may look like a duckbill, but screeching, whistling *Oviraptor* was a meat-eating theropod. Its name means 'egg robber'. Its remains were first found surrounded by fossilised dinosaur eggs. Scientists believed that *Oviraptor* had been stealing the eggs at the time of its death, but later discovered the eggs actually belonged to *Oviraptor*.

27

Dinosaur babies

Just like today's alligators or turtles, dinosaur babies hatched from eggs. Like alligators, some dinosaur mothers would stay by their nests to protect their babies, while others would leave the nests (just as turtles do) and the new babies would have to look after themselves.

Maiasaura

Big families

A dinosaur nest was a mound of soil with a hollow in the top where the mother would lay her eggs. She laid big batches and some nests have been discovered with over 30 fossilised eggs — that's a lot of babies!

Brooding mothers

It is possible that some smaller dinosaurs may have 'brooded', which means sitting on their eggs like a hen to keep them warm until they hatched.

Tyrannosaurus

Deadly threat

Hungry dinosaurs would steal another dinosaur's eggs to have as a tasty treat. Some, like *Troodon*, were quick enough to steal eggs when the mother wasn't looking.

Oviraptor

Leafy blankets

Some dinosaur mothers laid their eggs on a bed of leaves and covered them with more leaves. During the four or five weeks it took for the eggs to hatch, the plants would rot. This produced enough heat to keep the eggs warm.

Others, like *Tyrannosaurus*, would kill the mother or frighten her away to get at the eggs. Dinosaur mothers like *Maiasaura*, whose name means 'good mother lizard', guarded their babies and brought them food until they were old enough to look after themselves.

In the air

During the time of the dinosaurs, flying reptiles (called pterosaurs) took to the skies. Some were as big as a fighter plane, while others were smaller than a duck. Their wings were made from tightly stretched skin. Unlike birds, the pterosaurs were covered in a rough kind of hair instead of feathers.

Pterodactylus

Pterodactylus was the first pterosaur to be discovered. This small flying reptile used its jaws to crunch up fish and small animals with the help of about 90 teeth.

Pterodaustro

Like a flamingo, *Pterodaustro* used its specially shaped jaws to catch shrimplike creatures from shallow water. It had 2,000 flexible teeth to filter out the best bits!

Pteranodon

One of the biggest pterosaurs, *Pteranodon* had a wingspan of around 9 metres. It had no teeth and mainly ate fish. Some species had huge crests, like the one on the far right.

Pteranodon

Pterodaustro

Gallodactylus

Gallodactylus

Scientists believe this pterosaur used the teeth at the front of its beak to comb through mud in search of shellfish, or to grasp fish swimming just below the water's surface.

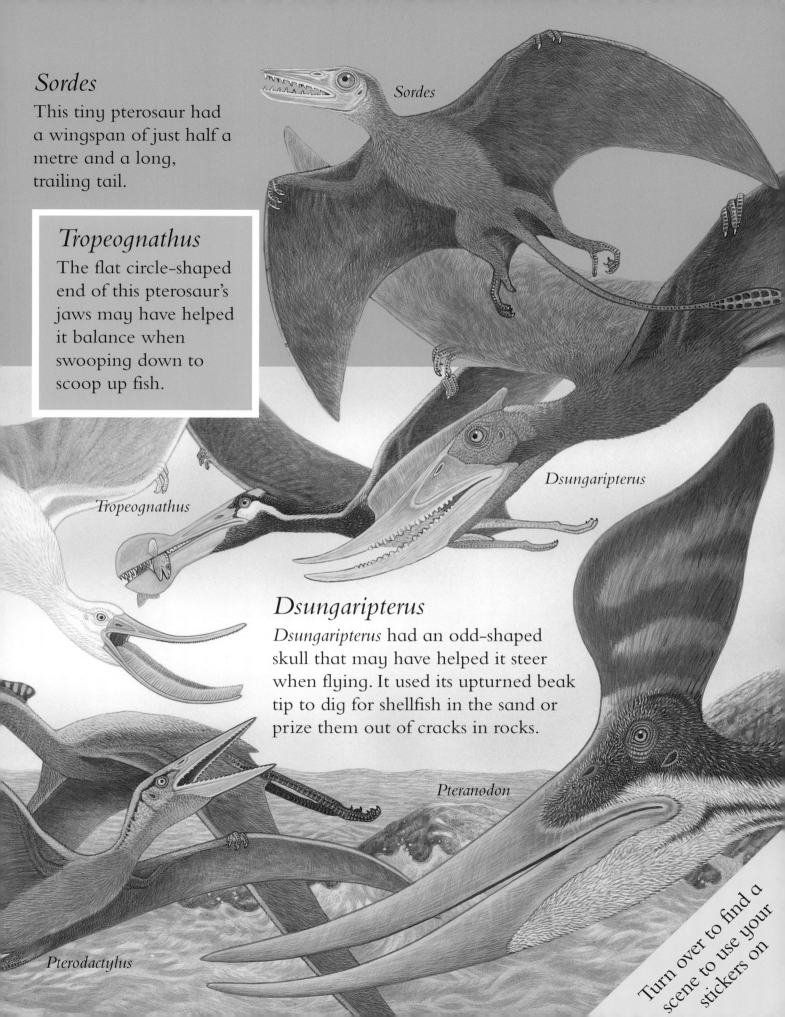

Sordes

This tiny pterosaur had a wingspan of just half a metre and a long, trailing tail.

Sordes

Tropeognathus

The flat circle-shaped end of this pterosaur's jaws may have helped it balance when swooping down to scoop up fish.

Tropeognathus

Dsungaripterus

Dsungaripterus

Dsungaripterus had an odd-shaped skull that may have helped it steer when flying. It used its upturned beak tip to dig for shellfish in the sand or prize them out of cracks in rocks.

Pteranodon

Pterodactylus

Turn over to find a scene to use your stickers on

How many pterosaurs can you add to
this picture? Search the STICKER FUN
pages to see what other reptiles you
can find…

Is it a bird?

The hairy pterosaurs were still winging their way across the skies when the first birds began to appear around 150 million years ago. With feathers rather than fur, the birds looked very different from the pterosaurs. Can you spot which of the two creatures here really were birds?

Mesadactylus

Eosipterus

Like many pterosaurs, *Eosipterus* fed on fish, although it was smaller than many of its relatives with a wingspan of around 1.2 metres.

Eosipterus

Mesadactylus

Mesadactylus was a small pterosaur that would land on the backs of large dinosaurs, and peck on any insects it found crawling on their skin.

Archaeopteryx

Mecistotrachelos

This lizard-like creature had a thin skin covering its ribs. When it stretched out its ribs, the skin acted like a parachute, allowing it to glide through the trees.

Mecistotrachelos

Archaeopteryx

Archaeopteryx was one of the first birds, but unlike modern-day birds, it had sharp teeth in its beak and claws on its wings. This feathered creature was about the size of a crow and is thought to have been more of a glider than a flier.

Quetzalcoatlus

The size of a small aircraft, *Quetzalcoatlus* was so big that it would have been unable to scoop up fish in the way that other pterosaurs could. It would probably have had to land to grab its lunch.

Quetzalcoatlus

Microraptor

Microraptor was the smallest dinosaur that ever lived! The size of a guinea pig, it had long wings, so that it could glide from tree to tree.

Microraptor

Gansus

Caudipteryx

Caudipteryx

Although it had feathers like a bird and was about the same size as a turkey, the wings of *Caudipteryx* were too small for it to fly.

Gansus

Looking rather like ducks, these creatures were in fact birds with feathers and webbed feet – they were distant cousins of modern birds, and are now extinct!

35

Beneath the waves

Life on earth began in the oceans and reptiles that lived mainly in the sea, known as 'marine reptiles', were closely related to the dinosaurs. Not all creatures that lived in the sea were reptiles and some sea creatures from the dinosaur age still exist today. Can you guess which creature here still lurks in the oceans?

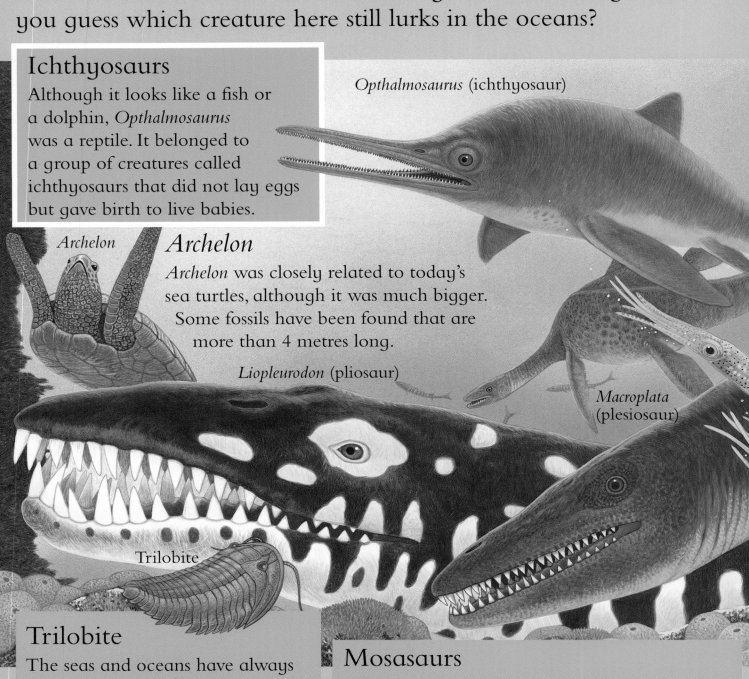

Ichthyosaurs

Although it looks like a fish or a dolphin, *Opthalmosaurus* was a reptile. It belonged to a group of creatures called ichthyosaurs that did not lay eggs but gave birth to live babies.

Opthalmosaurus (ichthyosaur)

Archelon

Archelon

Archelon was closely related to today's sea turtles, although it was much bigger. Some fossils have been found that are more than 4 metres long.

Liopleurodon (pliosaur)

Macroplata (plesiosaur)

Trilobite

Trilobite

The seas and oceans have always been full of strange animals. Long before the dinosaurs appeared, there were creepy-crawlies called trilobites. They ranged in size from 1 millimetre to 72 centimetres long!

Mosasaurs

Tylosaurus belonged to a group of reptiles called mosasaurs. It could grow to around 15 metres in length and was like a huge lizard with flippers instead of legs. It would attack almost anything including plesiosaurs and sharks.

Nautilus

The nautilus is a squidlike creature, which lives in a spiral shell. There are several different kinds of nautilus that still exist today.

Tylosaurus
(mosasaur)

Plesiosaurs

Elasmosaurus and *Macroplata* belonged to a group of fierce predators called plesiosaurs that had small heads and long necks.

Liopleurodon belonged to another group called pliosaurs. Turn the page to find out more…

Elasmosaurus
(plesiosaur)

Belemnite

Belemnite

Related to the modern-day squid, the belemnite was a favourite food of many marine reptiles.

Giants of the ocean

The creatures that lived in the oceans in the middle of the Jurassic period were bigger and scarier than any sea monsters you might have seen on TV or at the cinema. Many were far larger than killer whales, and there is one creature on this page that is still alive today. Can you guess which one?

Pliosaurs

Unlike the long-necked plesiosaurs, pliosaurs had short necks and large heads. The largest pliosaur, *Liopleurodon*, was up to 20 metres long – but it was no slow coach! Its huge flippers meant that it could swim and turn very fast.

Liopleurodon (pliosaur)

Horseshoe crab

This prehistoric crab can still be found in today's oceans. Although it lives in the water, this living fossil is closely related to spiders and scorpions. Some species can measure up to 60 centimetres in length.

Metriorhynchus

At 3 metres long, this prehistoric crocodile was slightly smaller than today's crocodiles. But it was a mean hunter – attacking ammonites, belemnites and even the giant fish, *Leedsichthys*.

Leedsichthys

There were plenty of fish swimming around during the time of the dinosaurs – meet the biggest fish that ever lived: *Leedsichthys*! This gentle giant grew up to 20 metres long.

Leedsichthys

Opthalmosaurus (ichthyosaur)

Ammonite

Hundreds of different kinds of this shellfish bobbed below the water when dinosaurs were alive. The smallest were the size of shirt buttons, while the biggest were as large as bus wheels!

Ammonites

Dinosaur d-day

Why are there no dinosaurs around today? Scientists believe that the dinosaurs died out 65 million years ago after a massive natural disaster affected the whole world. It is believed that an enormous meteorite (a large piece of rock) crashed to earth from outer space and hit the surface of our planet near Mexico.

Once the meteorite struck, a thick cloud of dust circled the planet. It is also believed that lots of volcanoes exploded at the same time, making the dust cloud even bigger. Such a thick cloud blocked out the sun's warm rays.

The world became colder and the plants that fed the largest dinosaurs could not survive without the sunshine. With nothing to eat, the plant-eating dinosaurs died out and without them, there was nothing for the meat-eating dinosaurs to hunt, so they died out too.

This did not all happen overnight but took place slowly over many, many years. Only the creatures that could survive the cold and change their eating-habits had any hope of survival. Can you imagine what kind of creatures were able to carry on until the skies eventually cleared again? Read on to find out later in the book!

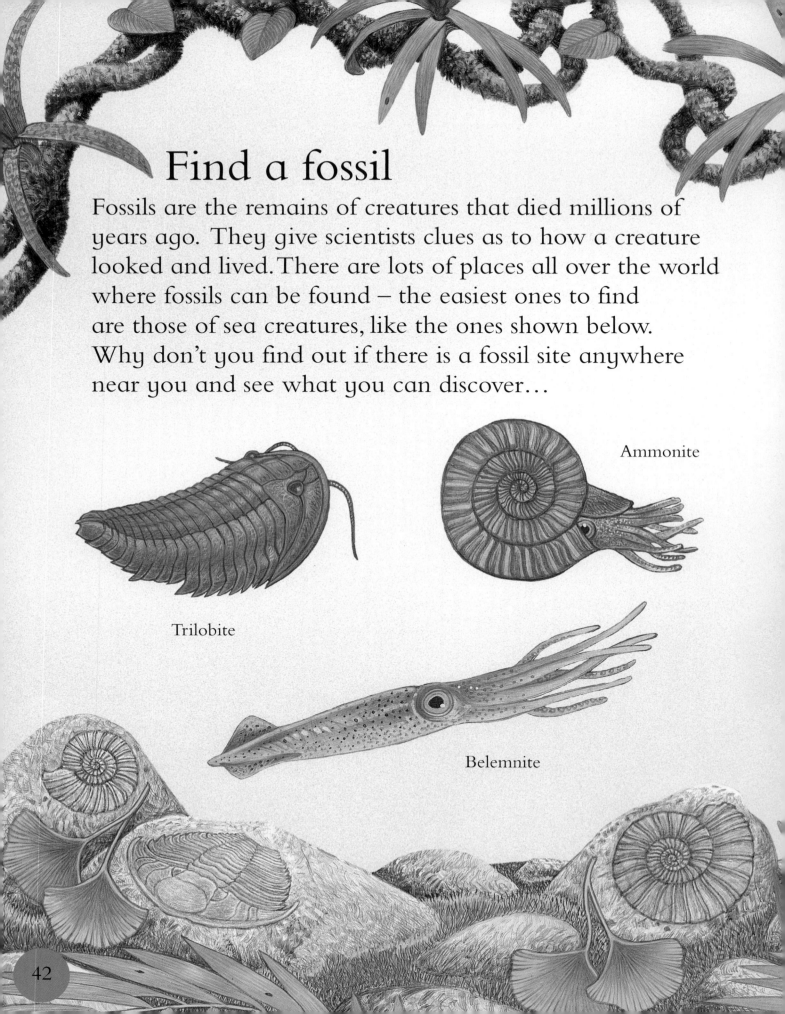

Find a fossil

Fossils are the remains of creatures that died millions of years ago. They give scientists clues as to how a creature looked and lived. There are lots of places all over the world where fossils can be found – the easiest ones to find are those of sea creatures, like the ones shown below. Why don't you find out if there is a fossil site anywhere near you and see what you can discover...

Ammonite

Trilobite

Belemnite

1. When a dinosaur died, it would often sink into the mud or be covered by layers of sand as the wind blew.

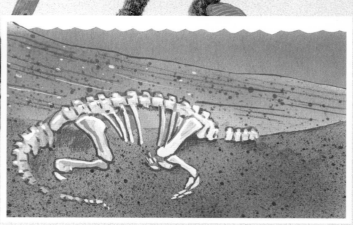

2. The flesh rotted away, leaving just the bones behind, as layer upon layer of mud piled up.

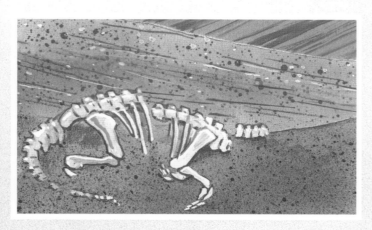

3. Eventually, beneath the heavy layers, the bones would soak up minerals from the earth and turn into hard, rocklike fossils.

4. After millions of years, wind, rain, river water or waves would wear away the top layers of rock to reveal the fossils. These would hopefully be discovered by scientists, or even you…

Can you find the stickers for each of these fossil stages?

The survivors

What kinds of creature survived the disaster that wiped out the dinosaurs? What could be tougher than a huge scaly reptile the size of a house? Some of the creatures who lived to tell the tale are the smallest of them all. Can you guess who they might be?

Sharks

The very first sharks lived in our oceans about 350 million years ago. When the meteorite hit earth, and the dust clouds caused the ocean plants to die, many sea creatures could not survive. But the sharks were unfussy eaters and would munch on anything they could find!

Birds

The huge pterosaurs died out during the disaster but many of their smaller, feathered flying cousins survived. Scientists think they may have stayed safe by sheltering in nests. Today, if you want to imagine what dinosaurs were like, take a look at some birds – they are probably the dinosaurs' closest living relatives!

Spectacled caiman

Morganucodon

Mammals

Small mammals, like furry mouselike *Morganucodon*, lived alongside the dinosaurs and survived the disaster. The mammals kept alive by eating insects or other small creatures, and lived in burrows that kept them safe and warm.

Saltwater crocodile

Insects

Have you ever had a picnic where you spent as much time fighting off ants and wasps as you did eating? Insects are experts at seeking out food because they have had millions of years to practise. While the dinosaurs struggled to survive, the insects fed on other bugs or dead animals and could cope with the extreme cold by hibernating (going into a deep sleep).

Crocodilians

Ancient relatives of today's crocodilians (crocodiles, alligators and caimans) were enormous – over 12 metres long and weighing as much as a truck – but it was the smaller types of crocodilian that survived. They did not need as much food and kept safe from the wild weather, by tucking themselves inside riverbank burrows or under rocks.

Cleveosaurus

Tuatara

The modern-day tuatara from New Zealand, is often called a 'living fossil'. This is because it is the only surviving member of an ancient group of reptiles. Can you spot its prehistoric relative, *Cleveosaurus*, crawling among these pages?

Tuatara

45

Dino quiz

Most dinosaurs weren't that clever. Many of the biggest creatures ever to walk the planet had brains that were smaller than yours! This dino quiz would have been a problem for them, but it should be simple for you, especially because you've read all about the creatures shown here. Just take a look back through the book if you need to refresh your memory. Can you find the stickers that go with each answer?

1. Which prehistoric dragonfly had a wingspan of 75 centimetres?

2. Which dinosaur had three horns on its head and 70 sharp teeth?

3. What were meat-eating dinosaurs that stood on their back legs called?

4. Which dinosaur lived in the desert and was up to 3 metres long?

5. Was *Diplodocus* a meat-eater or a vegetarian?

6. Can you name this sauropod that weighed as much as four elephants?

7. Which plant-eater had spikes on its front feet to gather food?

8. What weapon did *Euoplocephalus* have in its tail?

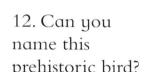

11. Which dinosaur's name means 'good mother lizard'?

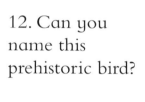

9. Which dinosaur had three large fighting horns on its head?

12. Can you name this prehistoric bird?

13. Which 'living fossil' is related to scorpions and spiders?

10. Which was the heaviest of all dinosaurs?

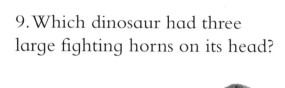

14. Can you name this mammal that lived in the dinosaur age?

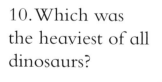

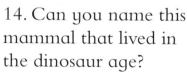

How to use your stickers

Look for the page numbers on the sticker sheets at the back of this book to help you find the right stickers for the different dinosaur activities. Peel each one carefully from its backing sheet and use it to fill in the shapes.

Whenever you see the words 'STICKER FUN', turn to the last section of the sticker sheets – here you will find lots of dinosaur stickers to add to the extra picture scenes throughout the book.

Soon you will be able to name all of these ancient reptiles. Then you'll be a dinosaur expert!

7. Which plant-eater had spikes on its front feet to gather food?

8. What weapon did *Euoplocephalus* have in its tail?

9. Which dinosaur had three large fighting horns on its head?

10. Which was the heaviest of all dinosaurs?

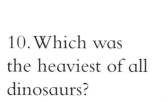

11. Which dinosaur's name means 'good mother lizard'?

12. Can you name this prehistoric bird?

13. Which 'living fossil' is related to scorpions and spiders?

14. Can you name this mammal that lived in the dinosaur age?

How to use
your stickers

Look for the page numbers on the sticker sheets at the back of this book to help you find the right stickers for the different dinosaur activities. Peel each one carefully from its backing sheet and use it to fill in the shapes.

Whenever you see the words 'STICKER FUN', turn to the last section of the sticker sheets – here you will find lots of dinosaur stickers to add to the extra picture scenes throughout the book.

Soon you will be able to name all of these ancient reptiles. Then you'll be a dinosaur expert!